KIDS IN HISTORY

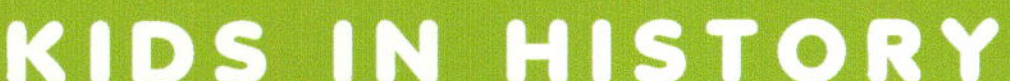

How Did Pioneer Kids Live?

BY MEGAN QUICK

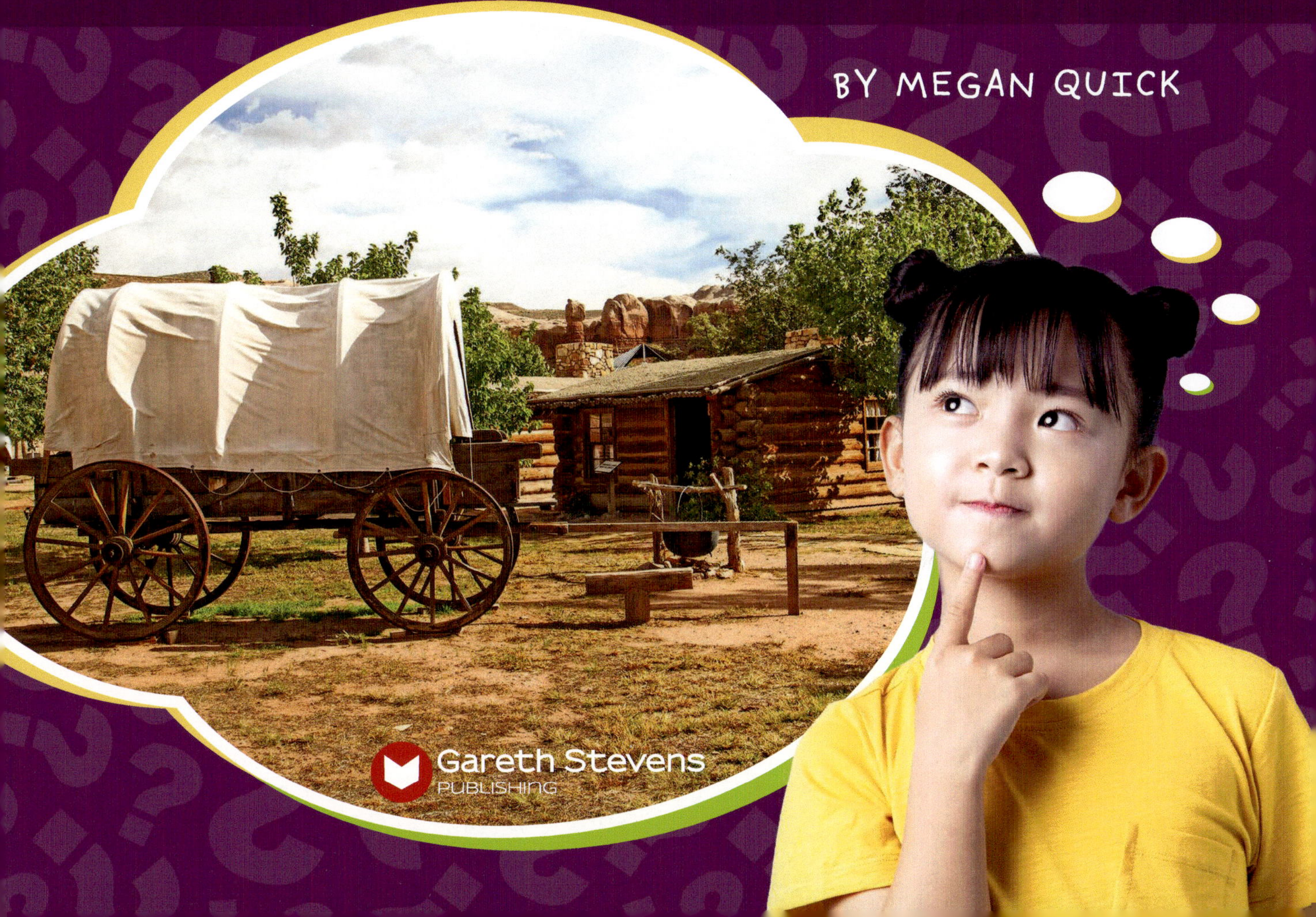

Gareth Stevens PUBLISHING

Please visit our website, www.garethstevens.com. For a free color catalog of all our high-quality books, call toll free 1-800-542-2595 or fax 1-877-542-2596.

Library of Congress Cataloging-in-Publication Data

Names: Quick, Megan, author.
Title: How did pioneer kids live? / Megan Quick.
Description: Buffalo, New York : Gareth Stevens Publishing, [2024] |
Series: Kids in history | Includes bibliographical references and index.
Identifiers: LCCN 2023012816 | ISBN 9781538288252 (library binding) | ISBN
9781538288245 (paperback) | ISBN 9781538288269 (ebook)
Subjects: LCSH: Frontier and pioneer life–West (U.S.)–Juvenile
literature. | Children–West (U.S.)–History–19th century–Juvenile
literature.
Classification: LCC F596 .Q536 2024 | DDC 978–dc23
LC record available at https://lccn.loc.gov/2023012816

Portions of this work were originally authored by Sarah Machajewski and published as *A Kid's Life During the Westward Expansion*. All new material in this edition was authored by Megan Quick.

Published in 2024 by
Gareth Stevens Publishing
2544 Clinton Street
Buffalo, NY 14224

Designer: Jen Schoembs
Editor: Megan Quick

Photo credits: Cover, p. 1 (covered wagon) Fedor Selivanov/Shutterstock.com; cover, p. 1 (girl) TimeImage Production/Shutterstock.com; cover (background), p.1 (background), series art (background) Login/Shutterstock.com; p. 5 User:Golbez/commons.wikimedia.org; p. 7 Everett Collection/Shutterstock.com; p. 9 Myotus/commons.wikimedia.org; p. 11 (table) Leene/Shutterstock.com, (hearth) glenda/Shutterstock.com, (tools) Evgeny Haritonov/Shutterstock.com; p. 13 Marzolino/Shutterstock.com; p. 14 Alexander Sviridov/Shutterstock.com; p. 15 bradwieland/iStock.com; p. 17 Paul Brady Photography/Shutterstock.com; p. 18 John Morgan/commons.wikimedia.org; p. 19 DeBevoise, C. Manley/digitalcollections.nypl.org; p. 21 Carrie A Hanrahan/Shutterstock.com.

Printed in the United States of America

CPSIA compliance information: Batch #CS24GS: For further information contact Gareth Stevens at 1-800-542-2595.

Contents

Words in the glossary appear in **bold** type the first time they are used in the text.

The Pioneer Spirit

In 1800, the United States was a young country. It included 17 states and several territories. But Americans wanted more. They wanted to **explore** and settle the western part of today's United States.

Throughout the 1800s, there was a huge push to travel west, all the way to the Pacific Ocean. Some **pioneers** set out alone. But many of these settlers were families with children. They went west looking for a new, better life. Let's find out more about life as a pioneer kid.

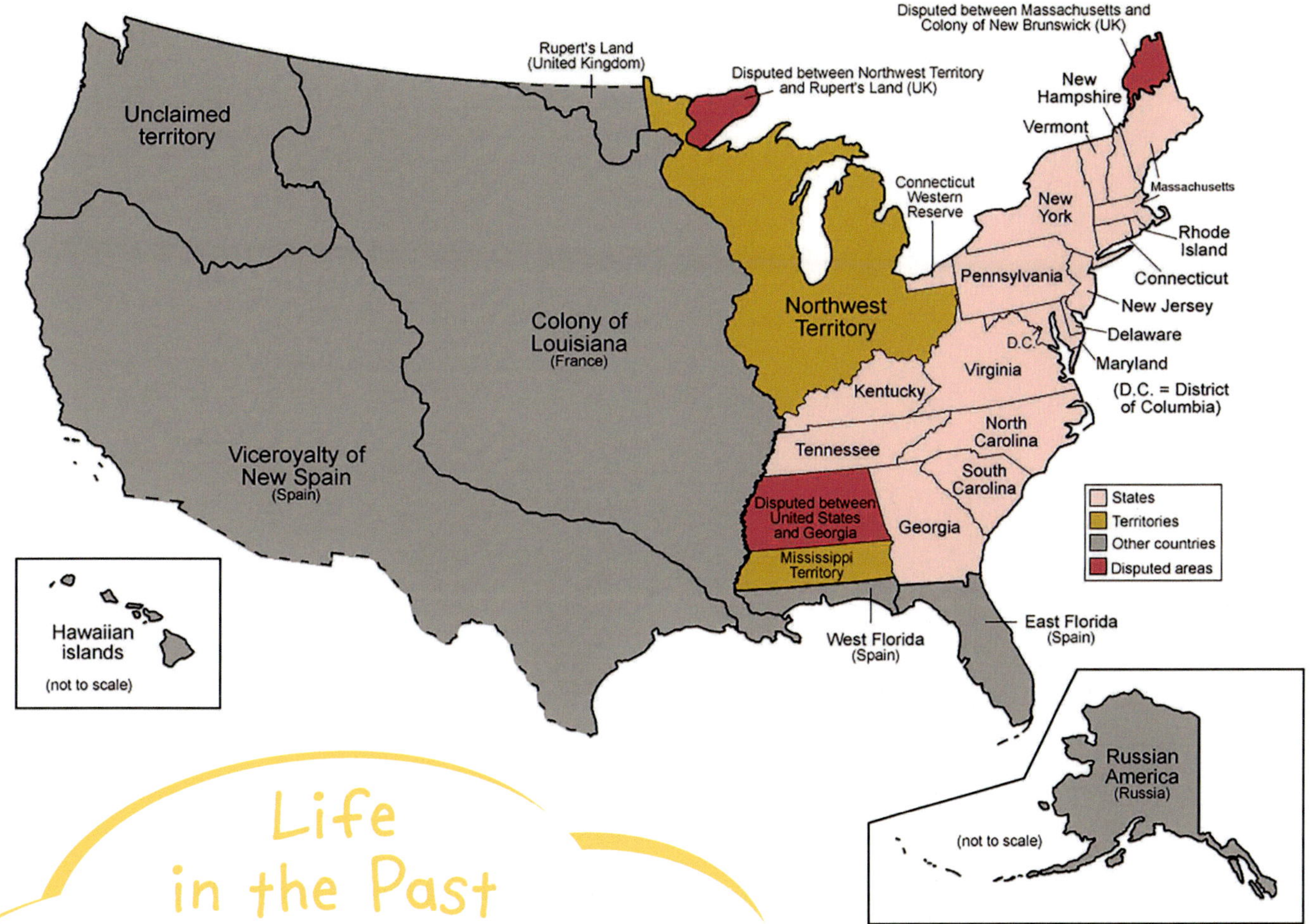

Life in the Past

In 1803, the United States bought more than 827,000 square miles (2.14 million sq km) of land from France. It was called the Louisiana Purchase. The land was west of the Mississippi River and doubled the country's size.

This map shows the United States around 1800. Most U.S. states and territories were in the eastern part of our present-day country.

The Trip West

The pioneers traveled across the country in covered wagons pulled by horses. There were no roads. The journey was slow. On a good, clear day, the pioneers might travel 20 miles (32 km). Children could walk alongside the wagons.

The pioneers often moved in large groups for safety. Wild animals could attack the wagons. The groups also traveled across land where American Indians had lived for thousands of years. The American Indians wanted to **protect** their land and their homes, and battles broke out between the two groups.

Life in the Past

Some pioneers went west when people found gold in California. They hoped to become rich. Other settlers were Black Americans who were newly free. They were looking for a fresh start.

Groups of covered wagons were known as wagon trains.

Setting up House

Once the pioneers made it to their new home, there was a great deal to do. They hunted and gathered wild fruit and nuts until they could grow their own food. They cleared out trees to plant crops. Then they used the wood to build log cabins.

Everyone worked together to build their new home. The men cut the wood in a special way so the pieces fit together. The children filled the gaps between the logs with clay, mud, and moss. This kept the cabin warm and dry.

Life in the Past

Many log cabins didn't have glass windows because glass cost too much. Instead, pioneers put **greased** paper in the windows. It let some light in, and it protected the family from bad weather.

This log cabin is a model of the ones settlers used in the 1800s.

Log Cabin Life

Log cabins often had one room for the whole family. The inside was simple, with a few pieces of furniture, such as a table, chairs, and bed. The cabin had a fireplace with a stone **hearth.** Pioneers used the fireplace to heat the cabin and cook food.

Some settlers built a loft under the roof. Children climbed a ladder to get to this open, upper-floor space. Several kids could share a bed made of **canvas** and filled with dried leaves. They hung their clothes on wooden pegs along the wall.

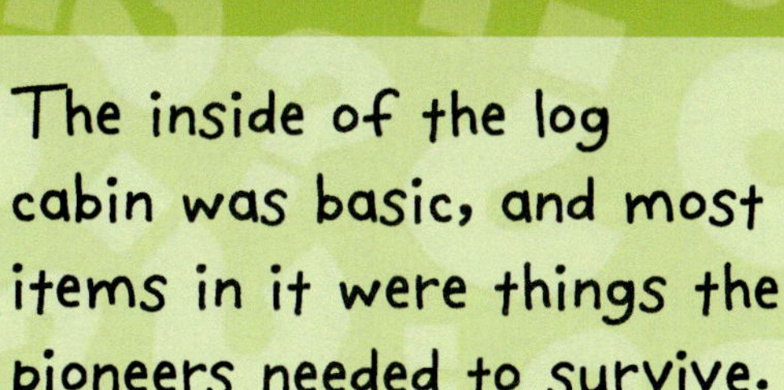

The inside of the log cabin was basic, and most items in it were things the pioneers needed to survive.

Life in the Past

Pioneer families were large. In the first half of the 1800s, American families had an average of six or seven children.

A Hard Day's Work

Everyone in the pioneer family woke early to start their chores. Children as young as 4 or 5 helped out. The kids fed the animals and brought in wood for the fire. They gathered eggs from the chicken coop. Girls helped their mother make breakfast.

After the family ate, there was more work to do. Boys might help their father in the fields. Girls made butter with cow's milk. They helped make clothes from different kinds of cloth. Chores had to be done every day, even on weekends and holidays.

Small children help their mother by gathering wood for the fire.

Pioneer Fashion

The pioneers made most of their clothes themselves. Children dressed in the same style as their parents. Women and girls wore plenty of layers, including dresses, **petticoats,** and aprons. **Bonnets** protected their faces while they worked outside. They wore **shawls** in winter.

spinning wheel

Men and boys wore pants and long shirts made of whatever cloth the women made. They wore straw hats when they worked in the fields. In the winter, they might wear a hat made of fur, such as raccoon.

Life in the Past

Pioneer families often raised sheep for their wool. By age 6, many girls had learned how to spin the wool into yarn that could be used to make cloth.

Young pioneers often went barefoot during warm months.

Learning Lessons

While pioneers settled into their new homes, there wasn't time for school. Parents taught their children real-life lessons. Boys learned how to use an ax and gun. They had to know how to make and fix tools. Girls learned how to cook and sew. Children learned the alphabet and numbers from the Bible.

When children were able to go to school, it was often a one-room schoolhouse. The youngest kids sat up front, and the oldest sat in back. Boys and girls sat on opposite sides of the room.

Life in the Past

Pioneer children didn't have paper notebooks like you do today. Each student had a small slate that they wrote on with a piece of rock or chalk.

This one-room schoolhouse was used by settlers in Colorado.

Time for Fun

Pioneer children had to work very hard, but they still acted like kids sometimes! They loved to dance. They played games such as hide-and-seek, marbles, I Spy, and tug-of-war. Girls made their own dolls from rags or corn husks.

corn husk doll

Families sometimes gathered for barn-raising parties. They **celebrated** with food, music, and dancing when the barn was finished. Women and girls also had quilting bees, where each person made a piece of a quilt. It was a chance to get together and share news with neighbors.

At quilting bees, women and girls could talk with friends that they did not get to see often.

A Growing Nation

The United States grew a lot throughout the 1800s. It added 29 states! Much of the **wilderness** in the West became busy cities and towns. By the end of the century, railroads stretched across the country. More and more people headed west looking for a new start.

Early pioneer families took a chance when they traveled to an unknown area. Even the young children played a role in building their family's new life. Together, they led the way for all the Americans who came after them.

This statue honoring pioneers stands in front of a log cabin in Ohio.

Glossary

bonnet: A child's or woman's hat tied under the chin by ribbons or strings.

canvas: A strong cloth.

celebrate: To honor with special activities.

explore: To search in order to find out new things.

grease: To smear with melted animal fat.

hearth: The area in front of a fireplace.

petticoat: A slip worn under a skirt or dress.

pioneer: One of the first American settlers to travel to and settle in the West.

protect: To keep safe.

shawl: A piece of fabric used as a covering for the head or shoulders.

wilderness: An area in which few people live that is not used for farming and is more or less in its natural state.

For More Information

Books

Goss, Elizabeth. *My Way West: Real Kids Traveling the Oregon and California Trails.* Berkeley, CA: West Margin Press, 2021.

Hamen, Susan E. *The Indian Removal Act and the Trail of Tears.* New York, NY: AV2 by Weigl, 2020.

Rusick, Jessica. *Enduring the Oregon Trail: A This or That Debate.* North Mankato, MN: Capstone Press, 2021.

Websites

Cool Kid Facts: Trail of Tears
www.coolkidfacts.com/trail-of-tears/
Discover more about the effects of westward expansion on American Indians.

DK Find Out! The American West
www.dkfindout.com/us/history/american-west/
Learn fun facts about cowboys, railroads, and law and order in the Wild West.

Ducksters: Westward Expansion: Daily Life on the Frontier
www.ducksters.com/history/westward_expansion/daily_life_on_the_frontier.php
Find out more about what it was like to live as an American pioneer.

Publisher's note to educators and parents: Our editors have carefully reviewed these websites to ensure that they are suitable for students. Many websites change frequently, however, and we cannot guarantee that a site's future contents will continue to meet our high standards of quality and educational value. Be advised that students should be closely supervised whenever they access the internet.

Index